# SINEW

## MUSCLE POEMS & MANTRAS
## BAR RANTS & BLISS

BY

## JOHN ARENDS

TIMELESS STORIES

ARBORETUM

SINEW – Muscle Poems & Mantras, Bar Rants & Bliss | Poems by John Arends
Copyright © 2022 by John Arends
All rights reserved

Published by Arboretum Productions, Saint Charles, Illinois

ISBN 978-069255410-4  (soft cover)

Printed in the United States of America

FOR

ANNE

&

# CONTENTS

*"I write scripts to serve as skeletons awaiting
the flesh and sinew of images..."*

Ingmar Bergman

&

## DIRTY SOCKS

My daughter's dirty socks
are grungy with the
mud and grime of
magic.

These soiled, sweet
sweaters for her feet
dance,

even as I lift
them from the suitcase,
a secret, errant gift
from the gremlins that sort
our family's laundry.

Within the worn folds,
the transparent webs at the heels,
the oh-so ordinary
polyester weave,
is the essence of
all that I have
lost and found:

Lost --
What feels like ten lifetimes
of watching her dance out
of the shoes of her eight-year-old
imagination, lost
to working late and business travel.

Found --
A toe-hold of faith
in the magic,
in the power
of happy feet
to heal.

## NEW MOON DESCENDING

Is it the Sword of Damocles
bent to the crescent of a bow?

Are the moon and Jupiter in tandem
training a star-lit feathered shaft
on the rhythmic soundless falling feet
of wolves sliding across a flat horizon?

Is the world flat?
Does Columbus hear in silent strokes of oars
the Norsemen's spirit call from shores of granite winds?
Does Galileo's right hand know whether his left
is friend or foe? Do the throes of gutted Nobel minds
enrich the noble turf, or despoil the soil with
an in-bred lust for mother Earth?

It is one question that is all questions.
There is one answer that is all answers.

It hangs above the rim of all horizons,
all romantic hopes,
all de nada dreams,
all things beneath the cocked bow
and taut celestial strings
that when plucked
by the hunter's hand
move men to cry,
loons to laugh,
and wolves to sing
in twelve harmonics
of truth,
of death.

## SKIN OF THE FRUIT

I'm thinking of the skin of the fruit,
the tumescent soft envelope of the grape,
the dimpled membrane of the strawberry,
the coarse coat of the cantaloupe,
the fuzz that is the fur of all fruit:
the skin of the peach, and its cousins,
be they tangy or serratedly sweet, or
drum-tight fortresses: the tomato,
the nectarine, the pomegranate.

Ah, the pomegranate, the poet's dessert,
that seedy fountain of lusciousness as only luscious
can be on the lips, the tongues, the tips
of fructose-sweetened fingers now
playing on the skin of the lovers,
now dancing along dimpled and swollen
orchards of promise rising into possibility.

Were such a feast unending,
were such goodness to be sucked into
the very core of the heart,
without being bruised by
knuckles of guilt or greed,
were such an appetite unfettered
by festering sores in the brown
cratered skin of mishandled affections,
we could all eat in peace,
we could all sink
the skin of our teeth
into the skin of the fruit
of human kindness
and feel its release
release us.

## CONSIDER THE ROSE

Consider the rose,
in these, the last dim years of the millennium.

Consider the rose
that sells for a dollar-ninety-nine
at the Citgo station, resting between
the holographic key chains
and the canister of beef jerky.

Consider the rose
that is lofted through
the mating dens and sports bars,
hawked as some cheap romantic hook
for the pick-up line.

Consider the guy sitting in that sports bar,
sucking down Budweiser, one eye on the big screen,
the other on a tattooed Guns 'n Roses groupie.
This guy is no horticulturalist of the heart.
But for $3.50 and a wink at the flower peddler,
he's suddenly equipped with a rose.

There oughta be a law.

This rose is no rose to my nose.
What scent is left is lost under
the cloak of cigarette smoke,
the fumes from the gas pump,
the diesel residue pooling
in the low gravel corners
by the highway stands.

The rose of the 90s
is plastic-wrapped, sterile, or just plain fake,
a symbol of the truncated faith in romance
held by the Uh-Huh Generation --
the Just Do It Romeos and the Gotta Have It Juliets,
walking uneasily, hand in hand,
toward an unknown, perhaps lethal union,
a union too tightly folded by fear,

never opening to the moment,
never blossoming into a living, breathing
transformation of possibility.

A rose is the very scent of possibility,
the shape of shapeless notions,
the furled, coy, keeper of secrets.

A rose should not be some roadside,
saran-wrapped twinkie for the heart.
It is not a thing to be bought or sold.

A rose should be plucked in the wild,
for there is, in its form, a gentle wildness
that rebels against commerce and convenience.

A rose is to be won, to be conquered,
to be had the old-fashioned way --
to be earned and worthy of the
most base and sublime urges
of body and soul.

For if you consider the rose,
its sensual, fur-soft petals,
its total embrace of color and hue,
its regal tilt atop barbed and glistening greenery...

if you consider its unfolded depths,
the dark creases curved and
moist with commitment,
with the urgent sweat of letting go...

you will find that a rose is the slow burn of love,
not the hot, adrenal rush of lust.

And if you consider the state of love and lust
in these, the last dim years of the millennium,
you will find that, alas,
a rose is a rose is
a rose no more.

## THE GREAT UNHEARD

Beyond the grasp of the ear,
beneath the ether-like net
of nerves that wire our bones
for sound -- for pain -- whispers
the voice of the great unheard,
the antediluvian hum that resonates among
roots and remains of ancestral memories
buried moist and potent
in the timeless peat.

It is the voice of species calling species,
being sounding out being,
that wild, serrated edge of song
out past the rim of human comprehension.

It is the voice of the bull elephant,
speaking to its young of ritual and survival
in grunts and whistles
ten octaves below our ability to hear.

It is the voice of the sperm whale,
reverberating black and deep
against cavern walls two thousand fathoms
beneath our desire to listen.

It is the sound a spider hears
when she splays her legs
and lets the generosity
of our grave and serious planet
pull her downward,
the dry white microscopic hiss of
her insides unraveling in
a whisper-thin filament,
that slender suggestion of a soul
out of which she weaves her home,
gathers her food, and
ties her very existence
to the out-of-the-way corners
of our two-legged world.

It is the sound we strain not to hear
as we pass out-of-the-way alleys,
or step over wet cardboard homes
and stone-heavy legs
splayed across the sidewalk,
the wet, black microscopic hiss
of needle piercing flesh,
the low rumble of tubercular cells
stampeding deep in the caverns of long-gone lungs,
the popping spit and crackle of hot-wired nerves
flaring behind eyes long dry of hope or faith.

These are the sounds that give voice
to the great unheard.

They are everywhere around us,
they are everyone within us,
to hear and heed,
if only we are
to listen.

# SOMEWHERE WITHIN HER BORDERS

**I.**

Somewhere within her borders,
Amanda lies down to sleep —
to sleep the sleep of
the living within the living,
the heavy sleep of two hearts
sharing the same blood,
the same destiny,
the sleep of a child
slumbering within a mother
stirring within a woman not quite
ready to be honest with it all,
not quite ready to confront
the unknown country
she is crossing into,
even as she sleeps.

In the morning,
she wakes and packs her day bag
for the quick, cross-border trip.
Amanda, you see, is a
corporate counselor,
blue-eyed and fearless,
the perfect lawyer,
the perfect woman,
the perfect instrument,
in her managing partner's eyes,
for the task of delicate disengagement,
of freeing the guilty from the guilt,
of settling a certain lawsuit
brought against a certain client
by the mothers of Matamoros.

**II.**

Somewhere within her borders,
Marisanna sings a psalm of fear.
It is the song of the matrons of the maquiladoras:

the mothers of the miscarried, the misshapen,
the children born with fist-like feet,
with foreheads broad and oddly sloped,
with jaws that click and lock
under the strain of common laughter.

Marisanna's song holds no laughter.
In a voice as round and brown
as her drum-tight belly,
she fills each room she enters
with a hum-like, rib-stroking
harmonic chorus of
life-within-life,
shadow-within-shadow,
mother-within-child,
so inward drawn is Marisanna's song.

It is a song of fear -- fear that her second
child carries the curse of the first.
In the morning,
she wakes Paco San Luis,
her four-year-old, milky-eyed son,
and stares down the steady gaze of guilt.
She cannot shake the belief
that it was she who failed
the almighty blessing of motherhood,
that when she left the home for the factory,
that it was she who fell
from the grace
of the womb
of the Virgin.

**III.**

Yellow dogs slide through dust and
rolling tangles of children
as Amanda rides through the
back streets of Matamoros
in a chipped paint cab.

She sees Marisanna framed
in a pepper-green doorway,
a wind chime dangling over her shoulder,
the heat and dust rising around her.
Her face is startling:
Eyes the bruised black color of olives,
lashes long and halo-like above
cheeks splatter-bleached by acid
and electrolyte and who knows what else
splashes from the open drums she wheels
each day through the factory
on an old hand truck.

The two women face each other
across the border of a small wooden table
covered by a green cloth the
texture and smell of wet burlap.
On this table, Marisanna sets
a plate of red beans, tortillas and rice.
On this table, Amanda sets
a crisp, white envelope.
Inside it are a new home,
running water,
clothes for the children,
a yellow blanket for the not-yet-born,
music, happy Mexican music,
Amanda tells herself.

As Marisanna reaches for the envelope,
Paco San Luis pops into Amanda's lap
and snatches it like a new toy.
He crumples the envelope, then snaps it taut.
His fingers -- all 12 of them —
curl out from the broken-backed crabs
that are his hands.
In broken English, Marisana asks,
"You work for the battery company, too, si?"
"Yes, they pay me for the work I do."
Marisanna's eyes drift down to her son, and she asks,

"Are you frightened for your children, too?"
Amanda blinks,
and hears the wind chime
toy with the silence of her answer.
Then, somewhere deep within her,
another chime sounds, telling her
it's time to run,
to the plane, to the limo,
to the mid-town curb
and the soft ascent into
the sterile, air-conditioned silence
of the law office.

## IV.

As words of "Well done!" fall around her,
Amanda stares at her reflection
in the office window,
at her own now olive-black eyes.
Her managing partner pulls
the slender stalk of a yellow jonquil
from a cut-glass vase.
"I understand you're going to have a baby."
He snaps the stem and pats it into her lapel.
"Congratulations!"

As the door clicks closed behind her,
as the light presses in from the window,
Amanda curls into her chair,
pulling her knees and elbows in,
drawing herself tightly inward
toward a faint fluttering,
deep in her belly.
It is the fluttering of tiny hands,
of tendril-like fingers
pressing against the border
of a newborn fear.

# THE RIVER ANNE

It is a river's song your eyes
sing at first light.
Like you, the river does not know
its own beauty, nor does it
hear the music created by the
unpredictable bed beneath.
As water through a willow's roots
bare in the sunlight sings in quiet
hiss-like breaths, then drops to
gurgles in a low chest voice
as it glides by earthen berms,
then pools in deep soulfullness
and soaks meaning and history
from the moist bark of beech trees,
you shape the landscape of our days,
cut canyons deep with the honest
weight and force of a spirit true,
and like your namesake, grace,
the River Anne becomes a river
through inexorable force,
molten in the early hour sun,
giving voice to light, to destiny,
moment by downhill moment,
exhilarating and urgent as dreams.

## A PLAYFUL GRACE FLOWING

Unfolding light falls on folded arms,
tucked under at the wrists, yes,
like cat's paws.

Rise of hips,
slope of shoulder,
arroyos of disheveled bed sheets,
you are a landscape emerging
in emerging light.

If land indeed breathes,
if in the hushed light a forest sighs,
if in dead of night in dead cold Greenland bays
icebergs groan beneath liquid skies,
then I, too, hear this, all of this,
in the subtle rise and fall and rise of you,
supine, unsurprised within this watchful adoration
over an altar alive with dreams yet to rise,
hope burrowed, patient and deep in the blankets,
and love all around and within,
like this light we lie in together,
one asleep, one waking ever more
with each passing rising falling entrancing breath
of you.

This waking, this awakening into wisdom,
feels like a playful grace flowing, and I smile
the same smile we send toward a cat, our cat, Bobcat,
upon his rising and stretching after a long nap
on the corner of the sofa.

We must meet each day like this,
thankful for the blessed light,
the upturned face,
the strength rising,
like your shoulders,
into the promise of this
ever-returning dawn
we share.

13

## BOUNDARY WATERS

The pair of lovers camped on granite bed,
encircled by water still beneath stiller leaf

and moonless night, awaits
the black-starred wings of loons --

messengers who skim not onto but
rise up into and become the water.

Surface and shape as one, they make
shrill music in midnight air,

pipe-splitting shrieks amplified by
a silence as immense as the borealis,

wildness exalting its wildness.

The two birds mated in songs that
danced across the chambered night above us,

the walls of our tent thin scrims in the wings
of a glacier-carved stage, framing

a *pas de deux de voce grande*,
two voices, one spirit,

one eternal night like all the others,
magical in its unendingness.

Would this primal joining of voices,
these ancient harmonics we shared

that night on the rock
last in the memory, in the body,

in the wild lakes of the soul?

Years later, now more firmly walled in,
I still hear their call, still feel your ascent,

as our private, two-voice choir rises once again
into the mist-like light of a new aurora.

## THIS VOICE

This voice
a lullaby learned in Germany now sings
beneath vaulted stone and arch in St. Charles,
Illinois, comforting the infant in all of us...

This voice
rises weekly in the raftered hearts
of Charles and Diane, elder neighbors,
always in the eighth pew along the western wall...

This voice
in artesian tones chimes dust from
bells too long silent in too many lost souls,
and so...

This voice
smiles as it celebrates itself through song,
at once knowing and discovering
its true Creator...

This voice
rises from a soccer mom soprano,
in some calling forth love, remembrance, faith,
in others comforting a more haunted loneliness...

This voice
has also been by weakness bent into obsession,
twisted into a siren's call, displaced in the ear
of an artist adrift...

and yet...

This voice
triumphed, and triumphs still,
rising into us, a silken wing aloft,
lifting, lifting...

# PRINCE HAROLD OF NORWAY VISITS DECORAH, IOWA

You held Prince Harold's gaze
for far too long.

You were only twelve,
yet years beyond as your eyes

returned and answered the royal stare
with fresh light from a kindred soul

who shared the timeless secret of
an unencumbered grace

born dove-like across
the cobblestone street

as if the crown prince spoke in the stillness
via the pivot of his balding reason for being

his receding relevance,
his hope, in you, a harbor found.

Passing by Vanberia's, the open convertible
glides still in your mind, thirty years

to turn a single corner,
the royal memory like an out-stretched hand,

palm up, awaiting yours to place and be kissed
in gratitude.

Did he have a mid-life moment there,
as you are now, his crisis confined forever

to Main Street, Decorah, Iowa,
yours to an unfolding future in St. Charles?

Humbled, he was, to see in white blouse and plaid skirt
a queen of Norway incognito among the crowd.

You held, then, the regal gaze of a crown prince
as you hold, now, the gaze of every man --

with becoming grace, pride, and a soul
who rekindles all our memories of dreams lost:

each moment rolling past,
the open convertible of our youth

forever turning the same corner, and at
which we gaze, outside of ourselves

and our lives for brief transcendent trips
abroad from body, from responsibility,

to a country grand and delusional and
over which our passions reign.

He was pleased by the way your gaze his returned.
He is seventy-three years old now,

you, at forty two, still his junior, still his queen,
still his lost reason for being.

## MOSS ROSE AT DAWN

As the moss rose blooms
each day, then folds back,
bulb-like, against the darkness --
or is it against the cold? -- it yet again
prepares its gift for first light.

At dawn, the coiled and
shuttered promise
of its soon-to-unfold story
catches the morning's breath
of moist light.

So, too, your soon-to-flower
at-rest eyes flutter quietly
beneath well-tended brows,
above lips relaxed, reposed.

Pale light and rising sky
usher the sounds of
our world waking up --
the click-click-click of
dog nails on oak floors,
the shush-shush-shush of
cat paws jogging on door jams,
the growl of garbage trucks,
SportsCenter theme music
trumpeting up the open staircase,
heralding last night's baseball scores.

The unfolding day awaits,
impatient, imperfect, yours.

If the treasures of an entire civilization
lay at my feet for the taking,
I would not take in trade their riches
for this sight of you,
for it is the pure essence of you,

unadorned, unawake,
all the more breath-taking
in that lack of awareness.

A kind and friendly artist
God was and is this day
for having crafted such
softness with such strength,
for creating such balanced
delight and mystery.

It is, your face,
in shape and promise,
both flower and flight,
moss rose and gull wing,
alike in elegance,
akin in its ability to lift
my heart and spirit,
whole and complete,
breath itself breathing
life itself into my day.

At peace against the pillowed softness,
the inner light that illuminates your face
fills our bed and my heart once again
with an ever-returning dawn,
private, protected, pure,
as you, the morning rose,
rise and greet the day.

## YOU ROCK

You
rock
You rock
You rock dreams
You rock old fears
You rock ancient rhythms
You rock in sleep
You rock awake
You rock

You rock
You rock simple
metronomic phrases
beat by beat by
shushing beat
you rock

You sing
as you rock
syllables escaping
in hushed high sighs
feather light in
darkened air
you rock

You snore
quite elegantly
in that same elongated
pause that belies
dreams emerging
to rock the night
away

You rock
the unrockable
notion that women
grow old unquietly, scolding
each lost beat of youth

as errant children too
stubborn to sit still
and not rock
like you
did
do

You rock
all silent chords
into cordial voices
the day-long stores of
moments easing into the
mattress of memory,
their slumber too
soon upon us
to share

You rock
as only a dancer
can roll her very being
into something larger than skin
and shoulder
and hip

You rock
to seek that
faraway cradle
called home, first home
a womb of music
laughter, love
life

You rock
it all back to
us, your creations,
your self-styled rock 'n roll
family, keeping your beat,
two legs, four paws,
four tails and
more

You rock
yes around the clock
to the click of dog nails
hard shoes, cat thumps
on oak floors, beds,
keeping the steady
beat constant,
assuring,
secure
like a
rock.

You rock!

# THE GARDEN DANCER

*For Anne, on Mother's Day*

Dancer-born, your fate as
gardener, teacher, homemaker
played out feet first --
calloused, blistered,
elegant, bunioned, ticklish.

The shoe racks in our house spill over with
black jig shoes overgrown with shreds of
silver grey duct tape, propping open the garage door.

Toe shoes from ballet now serve as paperweights
on Grandpa Jack's rolltop desk.
CD's more plentiful than mushrooms
litter the TV hutch and bookracks.

Music is as at home here
as the cats, curled yin to yang
on the rocker your mother restored.

You've grown to see the qualities
of these cats in your children,
an ancient grace,
compelling, self-evident.

Capless Advil bottles, ankle wraps,
more mismatched socks than we can count,
torn, many of them, from the teeth of two dogs
dancing the ancient set dance, Tug of War.

When dancing and love entwine,
music leaps from cat-gut bow and strings;
spirits join in, performing miracles
in three-quarter time.

Sunlight pirouettes across the dial,
as you dance before, during and after
each turn of each song, each child.

And as you nursed our first-born dancer,
stretched the arches of our second,
slapped mud from the cleats of our third,
your nurturing light dances still,
filling this home, this garden,
effortless as sky.

## DAN RATHER, GOLDEN GIRL

His life's work behind her now,
she struts on, insistent, insolent, before
the assembled throngs in the stands
held high on girders tempered with
wary faith, hairy trust and, yes, more,
sitting in judgment of an authority
without portfolio of violence or unspoken
acts of retribution.

She finds in this costume
an authority bestowed as
a consequence of awe, of
unblinking faith in what power
physical beauty and sunlight and audacity
can muster as the baton spins thinly into the air
between the 50 yard line and the press box.

She is antiquated, celebrated, held
front and center in polite goodwill.
She is institutional grace.
She is welcome
because the people wish to see her,
assess her skill, her composure, her dexterity
her anatomy, yes, and more.

She is symbol and sex and nostalgia.
She is heightened hope,
anxiety with a smile.
She is warrior in battle against
simple, unspinnable failure --
to drop or not to drop the baton.

She has our trust -- as long as she smiles,
every hair gelled in place,
teeth beaming, bosom bosomming,
cheeks cheeky in golden scaled arches.
America is born, lives, and dies within this smile.
Her celebrity, that amulet of desperate ambition,
spins in the ether above her, while
behind her back the entire band

high steps in time, hot brass blowing
against the grace incarnate
that is her lovely neck,
that is our freedom.

She spins our hopes, our faith,
at opposite ends of the wand,
buffered by simple knobs
of decency. Audacity.
She is our anchor, men,
to a distant moment only moments past,
when women objectified were unobjectionable,
and objectivity was worshipped with unabashed
certainty that truth will rise above falsehood
if you apply enough makeup,
enough centrifugal force,
and the center holds,
and the eye beholds
the glinting scepter
of fairness, of belief.

High in the press box,
gatekeepers of perception
dole out piecemeal flashes of fact,
sequins of truth, and illusions,
carefully measured and
sewn into place.

Dan Rather, Golden Girl,
high-stepping in wedge-heeled shitkickers,
his time in the late afternoon sun
more tenuous and insignificant with each toss
skyward of a rehearsed and choreographed agenda.

When the baton falls, as it must, will
the ripple of that moment propagate
past the sidelines, up into the stands,
and divide whole from whole?

Ah, he smiles. That'd be the beauty of it.

## BOOK DEAL

Carrying rifle, hand gun, grenade,
our shrinking violets are set ablaze
by willful tongues in cheeks not our own.
"Forgive me," lies dormant, alone,
in the minds of loving sinners.
Weep not for fallen heads of
flowers, nor state regret for
drops of sunlit rain
on petals grey as
wet concrete.

Opportunity is a dentist,
at the beach,
in armor white and sterile
and tissue-tough
at the seams.

Smile.
This is for the dust
jacket.

## CAFETERIA

*University of Chicago, Hyde Park, IL*

I just work here.
Carry the stack of plastic trays
grimy with Velveeta
through doors that swing hard
in only one direction.

I hear voices
on the other side of
the meat-brown wood,
latticed with iron stays,
opened to privileged minds,
wealth, and, well,
not a lot of the rest of us.

I just work here.
I just get paid here.
Proximal osmosis
is overrated as a force
for social change.

## KILL THE LIGHTS

Halogens, for starters.
Cool white hot
crystal gas arc
common worship
see more flaws
free!

Kill the deer-arresting
glazed assault on night eyes
hypnotized no more by
so-called experts thrusting
technology like a badge
into the faces of
authority-agnostic
dwellers in the
basement of
celebrity.

Kill the lights.
At least for seven minutes.
Marilyn needed no more
to disappear into the folds
of her white-hot celebrity
and vanish in the flesh
forever alive in the inanimate
iconosphere of sheer
illumination.

Kill the damn lights!

Let her, and spirit lamps
like her, rest in peaceful
darkness. Darkness I
can't find anywhere in
this damnitall glare
of hollowed-out
fluorescent
night.

## IN THE BLOOD

It's in the blood.
That's all we can say
when asked to explain away
the latest inexplicable act
from the war in the Balkans.
"It's in the blood."
As if the worn line
like a worn blanket excuse
will excuse and cover
the naked barbarity of it all,
the monstrosity of scenes such as this:

Three men in the woods north of Tuzla --
two with guns and a hatchet,
the third with no shoes,
a torn shirt, and his pants to his knees.

The hands of the refugee
cover his groin, the shriveled passport there
drained by fear of the very stuff the killing is about:
the blood. . . and its purity. . .
and who among the men in these hills
bears the scar of that first intentional spilling
of their own blood.

The warlord -- a pipe-fitter --
laughs at the cowardly size of
the poor man's offering of proof
that he, too, deserves safe passage
and haven among the righteous.
It is not enough. The warlord nods to his second, and
with the quick thump of blade through flesh
into the stump of a sapling the blood-quick cry shrieks out.

It is a cry indigenous to these hills,
a cry that, yes, curdles and turns the blood,
a cry that spills across the unanswering woods
and sinks into the landscape of this timeless,
this mindless, this most uncivil war.

For ten centuries and more,
it's been in the blood,
and now the blood is in the very air —
an iron fire of a smell.
Most of all the blood is in the words,
ripe in the jaw,
sweetening the spit,
moist on vows that hang
like over-ripe fruit on the foliage of vengeance:
hanging trees of retribution,
thickets of senselessness,
vines of unrelenting spite
rooted deep in the hubris of ethnic purity.

How do you cleanse the blood?
How do you purify bloodlines mingled for a millennium?
How do you scour clean this pipefitter's veins?

You cannot wash clean the blood.
You can spill it, splatter it, choke on it,
drain it, draw it ever thinner
but you cannot cleanse the blood.

So what is it, this thing in the blood?
What makes the temples boil,
the forearms swell above fists at the throat?
What makes the prong rise even under
the smell and scream of rape?

And why haven't we risen above it,
declared war on this agent of war in the blood?

I don't know.
Perhaps it's too vital
to the good in us, locked in an
unbreakable embrace that binds
us forever to this curse,
this capacity to kill that each of us --
*each of us* -- carries in the blood.

It binds us now to the blood running
in the foothills surrounding Sarajevo,
to the blood flowing black in the rain-swollen gutters of
Boybatton,
to the blood drying in the sun-parched sands outside
Mogadishu,
to the blood being scrubbed, even as we speak,
from the front steps of Public School #44
at 53rd and Homan.

All I know
is that it is centuries old,
and it is still with us, and
with us it will remain.

It's in the blood.

## THE LAST BEAR

The last animal to die
at the Sarajevo Zoo
was the great Kodiak bear.
He almost lasted the winter, before
slipping into a final hibernation,
surrendering to a strangely silent wind.

In that wind, there was nothing
sweet or suggestive of spring.
Only the smell of burning earth,
and dry snow, and nothing,
nothing that held the promise
of nourishment.

Before the keepers left,
the male lions had been slaughtered and sold,
their livers devoured for courage
by the local war council.

They say that starvation
is the most silent death of all.

The first to hear that silent death
had been the weak and the infirmed,
and the very young.
Calves and newborns
lay stricken in the straw, their legs
strangely disconnected from the
will to stand and run, as
disease gained a foothold
in the uncleaned stalls.

The hunters fenced off from the hunted
by only black strands of wire and an empty moat
died as they had lived -- eye to eye
and hungry for each other's blood.

The jackals, true to form, had
turned their hunger inward,
the pack imploding into a frenzy of
cannibalistic carnage, the
wild blood gone wilder still
until the last drops matted and dried
in the fur of the last self-mutilated survivor,
panting under the hot weight of the day
before succumbing to dehydration.

Everywhere in the scum on the moat walls
were shallow furrows scraped by tooth and claw.

Everywhere weeds were knawed
down to cracks in the concrete.

Imagine an entire zoo empty, abandoned,
without keepers, without keys,
with no open doors.
A zoo without a heartbeat,
without sound,
no caterwauling cries from the chimp house,
no whooping, peel-the-paint-off-the-ceiling screeches
from the aviary.
No plumage,
no rutting snorts,
no trumpeting,
no trilling contentment.

The zoo became not a zoo at all
but a museum, a permanent
exhibit enshrining the
relentless, singular pose
of death.

In water troughs
the rain water run-off gathered
old leaves, trickled around

fat ends of twigs
and slipped through the
brown gaps between
a dead monkey's teeth.

Higher up, on a sun-hot
slope of concrete, flies were
busy at the eyes of a leopard.

Behind a curtain of pig iron bars
the panther had kept trying to rock
to his feet, his insides empty of
all but what remained of his will,
that will imploring him
to rise and pace,
rise and pace,
rise and pace until the curtain lifts.
The meaty pads of his feet are still now,
cracked and grey with dust.

When the last bear died,
no wind clacked high
in the branches overhead.

When the last bear died,
no outstretched hands
bloomed with cotton candy, or
tossed soft white offerings
of sweetness and peace.

When the last bear died,
the black wings of his nose
flaired once, twice, then one last time,
searching the vague and indecisive wind
for the scent of food, of hope, of humanity.

When the last bear died,
no scent, no trace of humanity
died with him.

## LAYOVER BLUES

Footfalls find pleasure in the
polycarbon hard polish,
echoing through the citadel-like
sequence of glass ascending glass
that walls these temporary terminals.

We see too little of the people
always around us.
All this glass.
All this humanity.
All this invisibility.

Lust careens like a fly
in a glass box.
It settles a moment here,
on a pane there,
lingering on the smoked
plexi of the gate.
Then it's time to move,
gotta move, gotta catch that--
SPLAT!

Another wall of glass,
another cool Cosmo image
clip-clip-clips by in high-heeled
well-healed self-esteem,
into and out of
my life.

# HARD GLASS, HARD NOISE

All these intersecting lives
gathered around the luggage carousel,
a dance as cold as steel luggage
trailers in Chicago's gray wind.

The planes --
a curious, heavy noun, plane --
so much steel,
airborne, dangling wheels
somehow too small,
their diameter too brief
to roll the weight toward
weightless illusions aloft.

So much fuel to burn.

Find the normal man, woman
or child in these sleek hallways
hard with glass and noise.

We are naked in our travels,
all pretense exposed,
all rudeness at the skin,
all odorous attitudes
tucked neatly under
the arms, like the *Times*.

Find me in this mess
and shout --
loudly.

# THE AQUARIUM

They seemed appropriate,
the demons circling overhead,
as Kyle and I sat at the bar
in Eddie Chin's Cantonese Delight.
The golden tusks of wide-nostriled dragons
glinted not in the smokey red velvet light,
as two friends, long separated,
stepped back to revisit a chapter from high school--
a memory not written in any yearbook,
but tattooed, indelible and lurid,
into the skin of our friendship.

It was in Kyle's skin
I noticed most the
medication. Tonight
it was a puffy olive green
in the light of an aquarium
that shared our corner of the bar.
In sunlight, it flared to a
pinkishness that was somehow
unbecoming, unmanly, unnatural,
like the bleached scales of the
albino goldfish that drifted
in the center of the tank,
as if suspended by an invisible wire,
slowly turning to face each mirrored
wall in an unblinking pirouette.

Kyle pressed his hands against the aquarium.
Smoke from his cigarette curled around the raised,
worm-like scars that descended from
the meaty rises behind his thumbs and
braceletted across both wrists.

His palms flattened against
the smooth wall of glass.

"It's like that in there," he said,
starring into the watery realm of
silence and color and confinement.

The water was a translucent haze
of fine grained scum, the silver bubbles
rising like an unending line of
whispered broken promises,
breaking on the surface,
rocking askew any clear
view of reality overhead.

Each fish was a doubt,
Each fish a lover,
Each fish the unblinking eyes
of an unblinking parent,
or doctor.

Nothing passed between the
two -- the fish, the patient --
except a mutual respect for
each other's listless world,
a world where everything
has crashed noiselessly to a halt,
a world of smoky water and murky air,
a place of observers and the observed,
where the blood runs
lukewarm and lethargic,
and the gravel below shifts
only from the nuzzling snouts of
creatures who crave the urge to
bury themselves deep in some
artificial muck.

Kyle had gone nuts for
all the normal reasons
a 15-year-old kid goes crazy:
bad drugs, a fascist father,

an older girl more woman
than he could handle.

When the girl spooked,
and the fatherly advice began to draw blood,
and the turning on was turning bad,
he decided to turn off. . .all the way off.
And when he screwed that up,
he simply sank into the drowning pool
of paranoia and depression.

The fish floated as did the patients,
drifting through the hazy waters of
confinement, the time in days, weeks, lifetimes
passing with unrelenting sameness.
The day room was aptly named.
It housed their days,
provided a roof over their time.
Its walls held in the heat,
and made stale the air
always thick with the uriney smell
of self-contained thoughts,
and the secrets of cowards.

Kyle's eyes never moved from the
albino fish suspended in the center of the tank.
"The truest test of courage," he said,
"isn't trying to commit suicide.
It's succeeding."

The bravest person Kyle met inside
was Carlos. Carlos was brave -- and lucky.
He was in love, man, totally gone over
a 14-year-old girl who was gone to the world —
except to Carlos.

Carlos crouched on the concrete floor
of the day room closet all night, in the dark,

pulling out the soggy grey strands of a mop.
One by one, he braided them into a
tight, pencil-thin rope, the heart-shaped knots
of which tore the acned brown skin
under his jaw and grew black and wet
and held firm his last gurgling breaths,
the last twisted kicks in the noiseless
black box of a closet at 4 a.m.

Kyle and Carlos' girlfriend found him
half-an-hour later.
The girl, in a haze of tears,
wrapped her arms around his waist,
and slowly, tenderly,
added her weight to his,
pulling him down,
down, a quarter inch
closer to the floor,
so that he was surely dead,
so that she was sure he
would breath the vulgar
air of that place no more.

"It was the most tender act of love
I have ever seen," he said.
He was a lucky guy."

Kyle slipped off his bar stool
and went to the john.

I pressed my palms against the
glass, and watched the fish
drift behind the silhouette bars
of my fingers. . .
out of touch,
untouchable,
beautiful and grotesque
in their splendor.

## HACK POET

That Rilke would know,
Or Frost pick up tendrils of
fraud from beneath six feet of prairie...

Would the Canadians forgive
my cannibalizing poor Robert
in service of a populist angst?

Put a fork in it, Plath.
And Sir William, forgive
the lugubrious soliloquies
and mind the gap between
Yeats and Yates when
attempting to pigeon-hole
the underground reverberations
of my voice, tinny sounding
even when surrounded by
the ceramic vaulted ceilings
of my schooling,
the shower tiles of my delusions.

Peel away not one layer more,
odious critic, in search of
garlic sweet complexity
amidst the oniony opines
of hack reviews of hack poets
by hack wannabes.

All I wanna be is slammed
against the aural woodgrain
history of the Green Mill.
Am I sandbagging it, Carl?
Don't answer that, Marc.

Slumped shoulders
carry little for long.
Just let me slide down
the long doorless hallways
of my aspirations, lost
in the music that tap-tap-taps

on window panes of brick,
tell-tale reminders
that poets Edgar and Allen
ate and slept poorly in shadows
akin to these, words

never more scarce
nor hidden in the gaps
between each tell-tale beat of
this damaged heart.

Ah-ha! There it is, at last.
The buried lead,
the badge of the hack poet,
burnished and
embarrassingly bright.

The rest of you -- don't waste
any more time.

## THE CLOCK IS CRUELEST

The clock is cruelest
when it smiles in
humorous intervals
too short for the task.
Laughs as we run out of
time to heal the infectious questions
that are human longing.

A nuance at best, existence.

Ablaze with core universal truths,
time bends only for the mind.
We long for the bare-handed strength
to grip it by the throat and throttle it back
into sanity, into a measure more compatible,
more human.

Give me time.
You and everyone else
can have the rest.

## THE CLOSET

Rummaging through the closet of my failures:

The dust-grey shoulders of aspirations long still
stiff on hangers of disuse
the familiar clothing of half-assed effort.

See how the cloth, the linen,
holds the dust-settled air of confinement
within the woven loom of patchwork planning.

I was never a sweater of details, I guess.

In the pungent familiarity
of broken-in shoes and
holey socks of resignation
I find, if not peace of mind, a piece of...

Oh, never mind.

## CHOIR PRACTICE

Circle of strangers,
gathered 'round the fire of
reincarnation...

Cantor, please
carry aloft, off these shoulders
bowed in reverent collapse,
these too-cruel soloists --
anxiety and fear --

so that I may seek peace
in the music
of strange faces,
the snapping teeth
of unleashed dogs,
and the unity achieved
rarely, sweetly, in
a single voice
composed for and
created by
multitudes.

## THE MAN

Call the man my friend.

Keep the sweeping arch of
the arm as it encircles the
gray t-shirt of my shoulders
firmly in the corners where
treasured memory fights off
dust and dog hair.

Call my friend the man.

He dwells forever in
heroic light, not for bravery
nor chivalry but discovery:
"Ah-ha! We've found it!"
He pulled from a
broken-hinged trunk
the confidence that
would become
my voice.

Call the friend my man.

If you need to simplify it,
his authenticity will oblige.
Don't anger it and
never turn your back
on its good intentional
goodness.

Call the man, my friend.

I need his help with help itself.
Where did it go, all of it, all
we once and still and will
hold dear?

Call, my friend. The man

is dead. Call.                    *For Bill Meade, November 2004*

## AD MAN'S DEMISE

If I die tonight, will it be a genuine draft, cold filtered death?
As I head off to God's Country, to the land of sky blue waters,
will my passing be a productive, highly efficient death,
a state-of-the-art death pioneering new ways to die
with innovative features and death benefits
befitting a post-60's, retro-50's, hip-hop-hopin'-to-be-cool
90's kinda guy who happened to die tonight?

Will I croak with cleaner, brighter whiter teeth?
Will I buy the farm with no money down, 60-days, same as
cash?
Will I sail off on a magic deep-pile Stainmaster carpet
to the empire of the Almighty, with digitally modified
choirs of angels chanting asynchronously "5-8-8--2-300..EM-
PIRE"?

Or will mine be a boring death?

Will my obituary run short and bleak next to ads for mink
coats
draping the shoulders of impossibly long-legged models?
Will quotes from the Nameless Famous
share the same spread-ad space as sepia-toned quotes
from D.H. Lawrence and Ernest Hemingway
exhaled by a Brooke Shields lookalike?

Will the most unforgettable women in the world
wear black velvet to my funeral?
Or will Bob Uecher read my eulogy,
and mispronounce my name, even as he proclaims
that my life tasted great, but was less filling?

Will I be Kool in death, kicking the bucket
surrounded by white teeth and bathing suits,
bikini babes bearing silver buckets of silver bullet beer?
Will John Belushi lookalikes tumble down
the center aisle of white lies that was my life,
while a bimbo blowin' Bird out of a prop master's sax

hits the high notes of angst that were my youth?
Will Joe Camel wink at my widow,
while offering my youngest kid a smoke?

Will I die a long death or
will Death and I just do it,
'cuz we gotta have it,
'cuz we deserve a break today
from this freeze-dried death of a life,
this life with lifeless color
'cuz it wasn't printed on Kodak paper?

Will my death be the real thing?
Or will I just die a vapid death,
a silent electronic click of the remote
and simply turn off?
Or will my batteries be shot,
the batteries, alas,
batteries no bunny in a
pink pompadour and shades
would every buy?

And when I die, will this poem
keep going. . .and going... and going?

## WILL CALL

It's out there, in a slender
pocket-friendly envelope:
my life's purpose.

Can't seem to find the
original credit card that
made the purchase.

ID?  You kiddin' me?
Don't you recognize the
screwed up face?

Me neither. And
directions to the event,
kids, grandkids -- gone.

Is the ticket required,
like a coat and tie at
the Palmer House?

(My mom would have it
no other way.  But she's
gone, too, now.)

No e-ticket, no
in-flight movie,
no soap, opera, ovation.

What's the ticket worth?
Don't know. Haven't lived
the life nor rode the ride.

Let's be rid of one
thing, simple and clear:
it's my ticket, my life.

Just give me another second
to try and find it. No?
Uh-oh...

## FEATHERS LOST

I am not as old as men,
though men have aged me.

I am old in a moment.
Not as the tree grows old
with the passage of decades,
nor as a river is old
if it has wandered the centuries
to carve a canyon's walls.

My age is defeat:
a loss of youth to youth
as measured in tipping a balance
from dominance to deposition,
a lost battle from which
comes no rematch,
only exile.

In flight I am alone before
the eyes of those who watch me,
against the clouds a mere speck,
yet all who see me more than
witness my shape but feel
the weight of a shadow
rodents have come to fear,
by instinct more than experience,
for few frozen in my eclipse
have escaped the crushing blow of talons
that are chipped and broken
from rocks and branches
of mountain aeries.

I have mated often, though
each is as new as the first time
I rose in circled patterns
with a golden-crowned companion
whose feathers grew more ruffled
as higher above a canyon's cliffs we climbed,
until at least two thousand feet

above the rivered floor,
we hovered, danced, locked talons and
fell
free of fear
lost in a coupled passion
that gave weight and speed
to our tumbling embrace
of feathers and wings
that bent and strained
from upward rushing air
that roared in harmony with our free fall,
which all the while was
measured, controlled, and
completed in perfect exhaustion,
as we tore each the other away
and staggered through the canyon air
to rest.

I too have felt the weight of a shadow.
I have returned to many nests to find
my mate's brood of eggs
buckled and smashed
under the warmth of her own feathers.

I have fished the oiled waters.

And so I choose to be solitary,
my only companion the wind,
who is sometimes friend and often
foe, caressing and battering
wings that show in feathers lost
their weathered years of flight.

Now there is always distance in my dreams.
The wind from any direction I face is cold
from fruitless searchings for game, or a mate,
or partnership with another of my kind,
who in our common solitude knows
that play in aerial gymnastics

can last but an instant before we must
separate once again against the clouds.

Never, almost never do I see
a familiar shape, or hear
the echoed cry of a beak's song.
And often, when I am
alone and afraid of loneliness,
I lock my wings to the wind
and close my eyes to dream.

# ABOUT THE AUTHOR

John Arends is an award-winning poet, playwright, screenwriter and author. After earning his bachelor of science degree in journalism at Iowa State University, in Ames, he completed two years of post-graduate study as a recipient of the prestigious Pearl Hogrefe Fellowship in Creative Writing. In 2011, he was named the recipient of the James W. Schwartz Award, the highest honor given by the Greenlee School of Journalism and Communications at Iowa State.

John and his wife, Anne, enjoy life in the Fox River valley west of Chicago. He is an active supporter of Waterline Writers, based in Batavia, IL, where several of the poems in this volume received their first public readings.

This is his first published book of poetry.

&

www.ingramcontent.com/pod-product-compliance
Lightning Source LLC
Chambersburg PA
CBHW020606030426
42337CB00013B/1235

* 9 7 8 0 6 9 2 5 5 4 1 0 4 *